PAUL SHIPTON

Over the sea,
Just a little longboat ride
off the coast of Norway,
Is the island of Tora.

This is no ordinary island.
For on this island, many
centuries ago, the great Viki
village of Ulfhild used to be

Way back in the 10th century, Ulfhild was known as a noble Viking village.
The Vikings who lived in the village were known for their strength,
Their skill with weapons, And for their huge size.
They were expert fighters and hunters and could always be relied upon
by nearby villages whenever disaster struck.

And this was why Thor didn't fit in.

Little Thor Ulfen was not like
the other Viking boys.
All the other Viking boys were
big and strong,
Skilled with their axes and hammers,
And very, very tall.

Thor was none of
these things.

Thor was not big and strong,
He was thin and wiry.

Thor could not swing an axe
or throw a hammer,
He couldn't even lift them
off the ground.

Thor was not tall,
He wasn't even
medium height.
Thor was really quite short.

And so, because he was not like the other boys, he always struggled to fit in.

During mealtimes, he would try to eat piles of meat and potatoes like the others to become big and strong, but he could only manage a chicken drumstick or two.

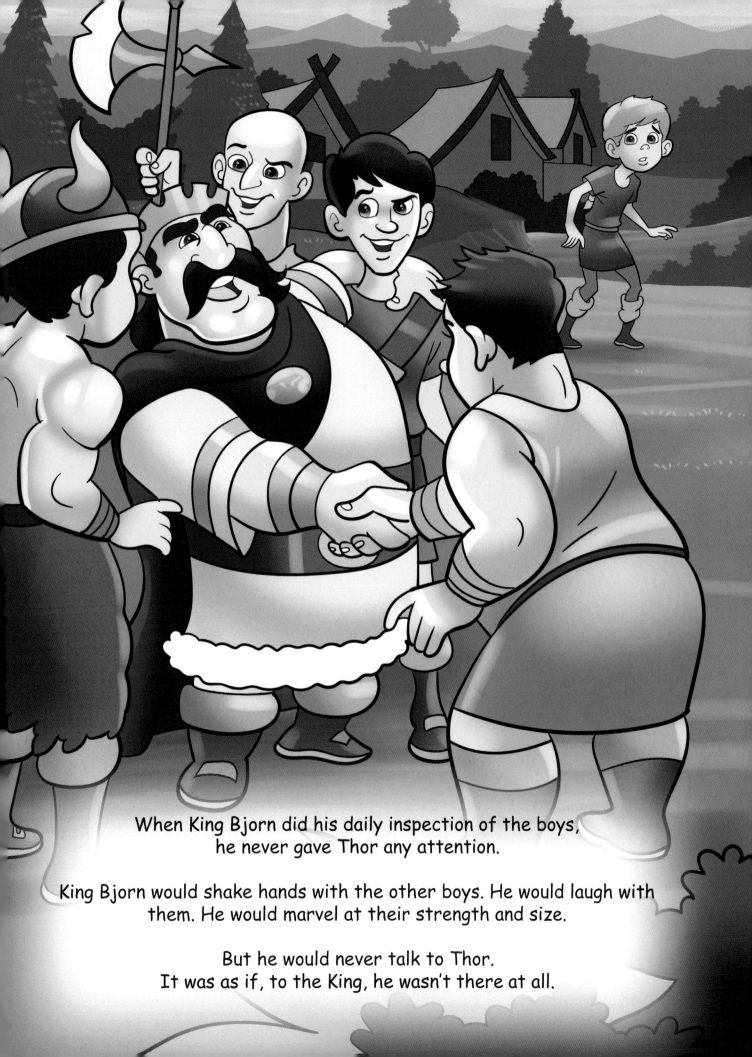

When King Bjorn did his daily inspection of the boys,
he never gave Thor any attention.

King Bjorn would shake hands with the other boys. He would laugh with
them. He would marvel at their strength and size.

But he would never talk to Thor.
It was as if, to the King, he wasn't there at all.

Thor's least favorite part of the day was fighting practice.

Every day, the grown-up Vikings from the village would take the boys into the woods for fighting practice.

All the boys would put on their armor, The enormous helmets and broad chest plates perfectly fitting their enormous heads and broad chests.

But when Thor got dressed
None of the armor fit his scrawny frame.

The helmets were so big on him he couldn't see a thing, and his shoulders
were so narrow that they would slip right through the chest plates.

The other boys laughed and pointed every time.
In fact, seeing Thor stumbling in his ill-fitting armor never seemed to get
old for them.

One day, during daily fighting
practice, Thor was having a
particularly miserable time.

It was cold.
It was raining.
The others were being
particularly brutal.
Thor was getting knocked
into the wet mud again,
And again,
And again.

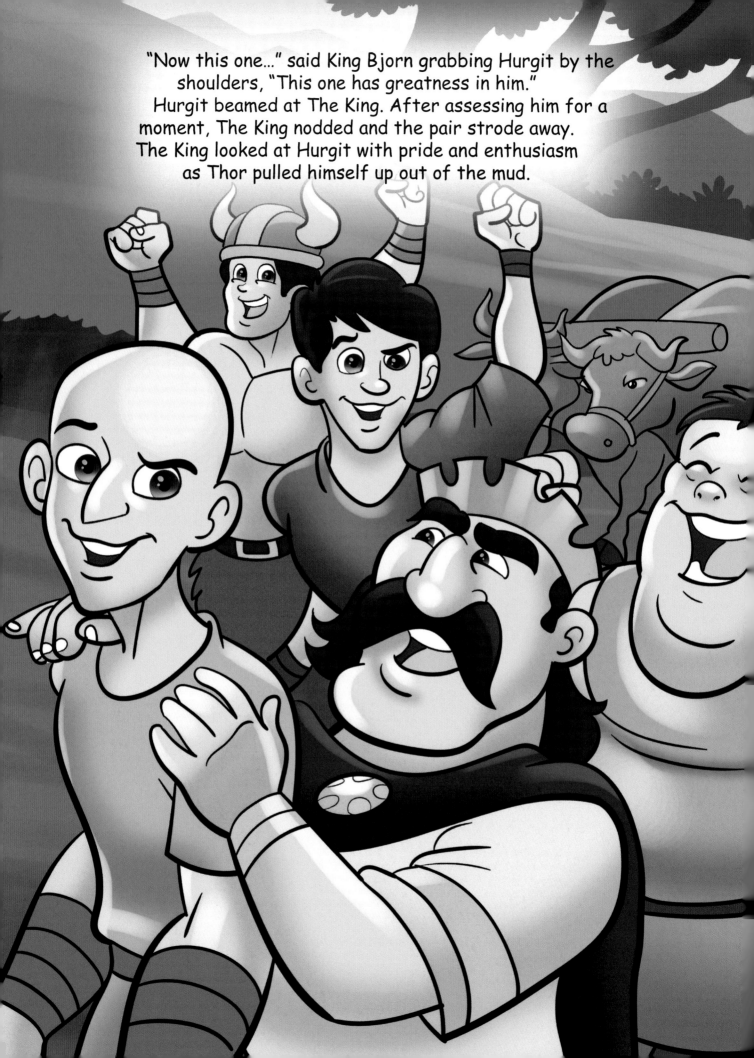

"Now this one..." said King Bjorn grabbing Hurgit by the shoulders, "This one has greatness in him."
Hurgit beamed at The King. After assessing him for a moment, The King nodded and the pair strode away.
The King looked at Hurgit with pride and enthusiasm as Thor pulled himself up out of the mud.

As the fighting party trudged back to the
village, all were in good spirits.
Cheering and joking after
a good day's training.
All except Thor.
Thor trailed behind them.
Slouching.
Sniveling.
Shivering.
Feeling very sorry for himself indeed.

The grown-up Vikings and the boys lit a big fire and decided to continue their celebrations by roasting a pig.

But Thor didn't feel like celebrating.

Thor slipped silently away, Without anybody noticing, And went home.

"What in the name of Odin is the matter with you?" asked Thor's father as he slipped inside their hut.

"I've had enough!" cried Thor angrily.

"Enough of what?" asked his father.

"I'm tired of not fitting in,"
Thor confessed. "I'm not
as strong as the other boys.
Or as muscly.
Or as tall.
I don't belong in Ulfhild."
"Now why would you think that?"
asked Thor's father,
sitting next to him and
putting his arm
around Thor's shoulders.

"If I can't joke, or fight, or even
eat as much as everybody else,
then I'll never fit in!"
"Well, I don't know about that!"
chuckled his father.
"What do you mean?" asked Thor.

"Just because you aren't like the others, that doesn't mean that you can't do the same things as them. It just means you have to find a different way. Your own way," explained his father.

"Do you see?" explained Thor's father. "You may not be tall, Or muscly, Or strong. But you have other skills."

"You are small, which means that you can hide and go unnoticed. You are fast, which means that you can catch people up more easily. You are light, which means that you can climb trees to look out for things and go where others dare not. And as for weapons, well, it's time I gave you this..."

Thor's father walked over to a wooden box in the corner
and pulled out a beautiful bow, made of silver birch.
The curve of the bow shone in the firelight.

"This was my first bow," he explained. "My grandfather made
it for me himself. I have been waiting for the right time to
pass it down to you. Now is that time.
Remember, everybody has something special to give.
You were named after the God of Thunder.
He never gave up And neither should you."

Thor was woken next morning
by shouting.
"My boy!" King Bjorn's voice yelled
from outside. "Help! He's kidnapped
my boy. Somebody stop him!"
Thor rushed outside so see what
was happening. In the distance,
a huge man was sprinting away from
the village, the King's baby son
in his arms.

All of the Viking boys had gathered outside now.
"It's one of those blasted soldiers from the village across the lake!
He's taken my boy for ransom! Don't just stand there. Go!" bellowed King Bjorn.

And so, every boy grabbed their weapon and sprinted after the thief.
Thor ran as fast as his skinny legs could carry him with his bow in hand.

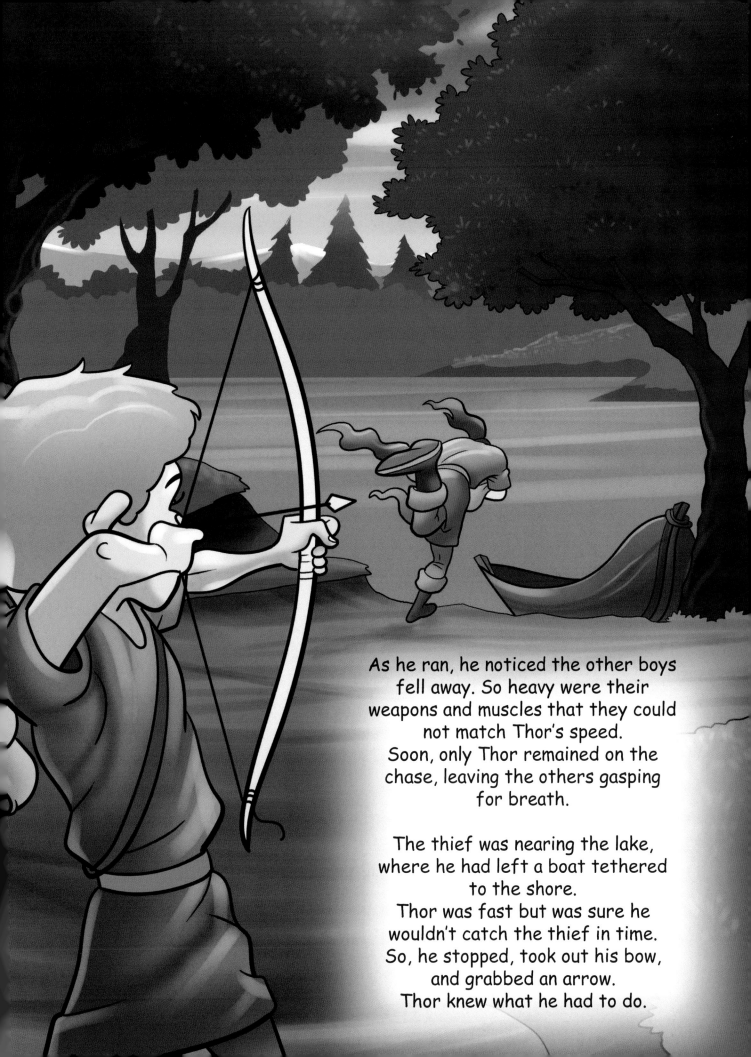

As he ran, he noticed the other boys fell away. So heavy were their weapons and muscles that they could not match Thor's speed.
Soon, only Thor remained on the chase, leaving the others gasping for breath.

The thief was nearing the lake, where he had left a boat tethered to the shore.
Thor was fast but was sure he wouldn't catch the thief in time.
So, he stopped, took out his bow, and grabbed an arrow.
Thor knew what he had to do.

Just as the thief arrived at his boat,
an arrow whistled past him.
The arrow pierced straight through the twine
tying the boat to the shore, setting it adrift.
The thief looked around frantically, but there
was nothing he could do. He was trapped.

Thor watched proudly from the distance as
the King's men rode past him on horses,
closing in on the helpless thief.

As the Vikings returned to the village with the thief in chains, they cheered and clapped for Thor.
King Bjorn put his arm around Thor's tiny shoulder, looked down at him and said, "Well, it looks like I was wrong about you, young man!"

Later that night, as celebrations took place around the village fire, his father came to sit next to him.

"You see," he said, hugging his son. "I knew you'd find a way if you kept going." "Only quitters quit," smiled Thor.
"Well said," replied his father. "All caterpillars turn into butterflies, and no two butterflies are the same. But all butterflies are beautiful."

THE END